PURE PLANET PRODUCTS®

PRESENTS

—SPIRULINA—

POWER HEALTH

HANDBOOK

for Optimal Nutrition

and Maximum Energy

Pure Planet Products

2945 Southwest Drive Sedona, AZ 86336

P.O. Box 3054 W. Sedona, AZ 86340

(520) 204-1806   Fax (520) 204-1434

www.pureplanet.com   e-mail: pureplan@sedona.net

DOCTOR TESTIMONIALS:

I have been using Pure Planet Products for many years for myself, family and patients. As a doctor utilizing applied kinesiology, I have subjected these products to blind testing versus other spirulinas and other forms of algae. I feel this product is the best algae product available today. I am very excited about Pure Planet's new Supernatural Meal. I had some input into its formulation and as a quick meal or something to take backpacking or camping, it is ideal and the quality of the ingredients, in my opinion, far surpasses that of similar products.
Michael Lebowitz, DC

In my naturopathic medical practice I am always searching for products of potency and quality for my patients. Many times I must make and formulate my own products. Pure Planet is one of the few companies I can trust to maintain the levels of purity and quality I demand. Spirulina is a whole food that forms the basis of a good nutritional program. I often use it as a reliable source of natural beta carotene. Vegetarians particularly benefit because it provides protein and vitamin B12.
Silena Heron, N.D.

ACKNOWLEDGMENTS:

We wish to gratefully acknowledge the following individuals for their assistance in proofreading and editing the Power Health Handbook: Ed Barattini, Heidi Benson, Carol Gillette, Robin Keenan, Mica LaBellarte, Mollie McCarthy, Robert "Desert" Nichols, Angela Parker, and Mei Wei Wong.

Contents

1. Spirulina: An Ancient Gift from the Earth—Rediscovered *1*

2. From Sacred Power Plant of the Aztecs to Space-Age Food for NASA . . *2*

3. What Makes Spirulina So Remarkable? *3*

4. Shortened Typical Analysis *8*

5. Spirulina & the Environment *9*

6. How Does Spirulina Compare with the Other Green Superfoods? *13*

7. Growing Process for Pure Planet® Spirulina *15*

8. Building Our Immune System with Pure Planet® Spirulina *17*

9. Spirulina for Athletes & Bodybuilders *24*

10. Slimming with Spirulina *28*

11. Spirulina and Pregnancy *33*

12. Spirulina and Children *33*

13. Spirulina and Animals *37*

14. Pure Planet Products®: *39*

    Pure Planet® 100% Pure Spirulina™:
    World's Only 100% Pure Tablet *39*

    Pure Planet® Power Carob-Mint Spirulina™:
    Delicious Instant Energy *39*

    Ester-C® PLUS™: *The Ultimate Vitamin C* *42*

    Ginseng Plus™:
    The King of Herbs Meets the Sacred Power Food of the Aztecs *43*

    Amla-C Plus™:
    Nature's Most Potent Source of Vitamin C *45*

    The Supernatural Meal™:
    World's First Complete & Natural Green Feast in a Drink *46*

15. Pure Planet® Spirulina Recipes *49*

    Bibliography *55*

Why is spirulina called blue-green algae?

The blue refers to the blue pigment, a protein called
phycocyanin. The green pigment is chlorophyll
which helps plant cells capture and convert sunlight
into energy. Chlorophyll is nearly identical
in molecular structure to human red blood cells
and is often referred to as green blood.

I

An Ancient Gift
from the Earth—Rediscovered

N THIS AGE OF NUTRITIONAL AWARENESS and health
consciousness, the search for the perfect food has
led to an amazing vegetable microorganism called
spirulina. Spirulina is nature's most nutritious
whole food. Containing hundreds of nutrients, all working
synergistically to maximize potency and effectiveness, spirulina is the most complete source of total nutrition on Earth.

This modern miracle plant is actually as old as the Earth
itself. It occupies a unique biological niche in the plant kingdom. Spirulina is a blue-green algae, a microscopic fresh-
water plant descended from the world's first photosynthetic life
form. It is composed of transparent, bubble-thin cells stacked
end-to-end forming a spiral filament. What makes spirulina
truly unique from other foods is that all the nutrition contained
in this miracle plant is easily and totally digestible.

2

From Sacred Power Plant
of the Aztecs to Space-age Food for NASA

NCIENT CULTURES WERE AWARE of spirulina as an exceptional, life-generating food source and held its remarkable energizing and rejuvenating properties in high esteem. The Aztecs considered it a Sacred Power Plant. Priests and warriors sustained themselves (at times, solely) on dried spirulina wafers. In 1980, when spirulina was first made commercially available, it was called the food of the future. NASA has chosen spirulina as an ideal food to grow on space stations. It is the most efficient, oxygen-generating, high-potency food known.

Today, spirulina has become an essential part of the diet of millions of people around the world. The annual human consumption of cultivated spirulina currently exceeds 2,000 metric tons. Such a rapid acceptance of a new food is without precedence and is mainly due to the wondrous properties of this power food.

In the following pages you will discover the many benefits of spirulina. It is difficult to adequately describe spirulina with words such as food or even medicine. For example, thirty-five children in Russia who suffered radiation poisoning as a result of the Chernobyl disaster were fed five grams of spirulina daily. They made dramatic recoveries within six weeks while other children in the control group who were not given spirulina remained ill. Based on this, spirulina is approved in Russia as a "medicine food."

3
What Makes Spirulina So Remarkable?

A Total Food

PIRULINA CONTAINS ALL of the nutrients the body needs, not just vitamins and minerals. In a retreat on Mt. Hakone near Tokyo, Japanese philosopher Toru Matsui is reported to have lived for seventeen years exclusively on spirulina. One could not subsist solely on vitamin and mineral supplements. He is living proof that spirulina is a complete food for human nutrition.

The Natural Alternative

SPIRULINA OFFERS the most complete and potent natural food supplement today. With store shelves stocked with so many brands of multiple vitamin/mineral supplements, one might be surprised to learn that most of them are laboratory-synthesized chemical compounds. Much of the research today demonstrates increased stress on organs and the decreased absorption of synthetic compounds as compared to natural sources. In the words of internationally acclaimed author and nutritionist Dr. Paavo Airola: "It is wisest and safest to take vitamins and minerals in the form of food supplements where they occur in their natural form and strength, and in combination with all of the other nutritive factors such as enzymes and trace elements, for optimum assimilation and biological activity."

A Superior Source of Biological Protein

NOT ALL PROTEINS ARE CREATED EQUAL. The proteins in spirulina are absolutely unique and particularly suited for the nutritional needs of the human body. Other plant proteins are notably low in biological value because of incomplete essential amino acids. Spirulina is a high-biological value protein with a superior, complete amino acid profile which contains in the correct proportions all eight essential amino acids plus an additional ten nonessential amino acids. Animal proteins are complete proteins like spirulina and they are of questionable quality because of their: (1) high levels of saturated fats and cholesterol, and (2) high residues of toxic pesticides, herbicides, drugs and hormones. Spirulina contains no saturated fats. It is remarkably low in calories and is free of cholesterol. Moreover, spirulina contains no poisons or toxic chemical residues. In fact, the United Nations conducted a five-year toxicology study on spirulina and found it to be completely non-toxic. It is also one of the only (if not the only) non-mucus-forming and non-acid-forming proteins.

Superior Assimilation and Digestibility

Spirulina is so easily digestible that no laboratory synthesizing is required to extract its nutrients. Spirulina's cell walls are bubble-thin mucopolysaccharides (complex natural sugars) which dissolve upon contact with moisture and digestive enzymes. Other plant foods have nutrients which are largely unavailable (unless cooked or sprouted) because they are encased like microscopic nuts within walls of tough indigestible cellulose. Spirulina, on the other hand, has unmatched digestibility. Its amino acids are delivered in an essentially free form state for instantaneous assimilation. Within moments, its concentrated nutrients, enzymes, and living essences are absorbed into the bloodstream without the momentous loss of energy incurred in the digestion of ordinary foods. Other high protein foods are characteristically difficult to digest (e.g., beef, chicken, fish, milk).

Dynamic Energy and Endurance

NUTRITIONALLY ENLIGHTENED fitness enthusiasts, bodybuilders, professional coaches, and competitive athletes who use spirulina are experiencing exciting performance improvements.

They report increased energy and enhanced endurance. Hundreds of Olympic and world champion athletes are using spirulina both during training and competition. Olympian Lee Evans, double gold medalist and holder of four world records in track and field, says, "Spirulina improved my training, resulting in faster times (and it) increased my stamina and endurance." Now as a coach, Lee insists all his athletes use spirulina. People suffering from Chronic Fatigue Syndrome and hypoglycemia also report a significant increase in their energy levels and overall vitality from regular use of spirulina.

Leanness and Aliveness

DOCTORS, NATUROPATHS, CLINICIANS and dieters are discovering the remarkably effective spirulina way to leanness and aliveness. Spirulina offers a natural, easy way to stay fit and trim while maintaining a high energy level, without the physical and mental exertion, stress or strain often associated with most fitness regimes and weight-reduction programs. Spirulina's supernutrition satisfies hunger because it fulfills the body's biochemical needs. The surprising success of spirulina seems to be in its ability to facilitate low-calorie eating without the energy-draining and health-destroying nutritional deficiencies that underlie the failures of most weight-reduction programs. And since spirulina is one of nature's richest sources of phenylalanine, dieters claim that spirulina effectively suppresses their appetite and boosts their energy levels.

Nature's Richest Whole Food

SPIRULINA NATURALLY CONTAINS some of the highest amounts of the following nutrients ever found in foods:

Spirulina is a rich whole-food source of Vitamin B_{12}. Fifteen tablets of Pure Planet® Spirulina provides more B_{12} than a serving of fish or eggs. B_{12} is essential for maintaining energy and healthy blood.

Spirulina is nature's richest whole-food source of biochelated organic iron. Six tablets of Pure Planet® Spirulina provides as much iron as 80 grams of liver or nearly two cups of fresh spinach.

Spirulina is nature's richest whole-food source of Vitamin E. It is three times richer than raw wheat germ and its biological activity is 49% greater than synthetic vitamin E.

Spirulina is nature's richest whole-food source of the antioxidant beta carotene (pro-Vitamin A). Antioxidants are nutrients which help minimize oxidative damage caused by toxic free radicals. Spirulina provides beta carotene (in four different molecular forms) in a naturally chelated food matrix which is more easily absorbed than the beta carotene in broccoli and carrots. Six tablets of spirulina provides nearly twice the beta carotene of one medium carrot. Unlike the pre-formed vitamin A of synthetics and fish liver oils, beta carotene is completely nontoxic even in megadoses.

Spirulina is rich in whole-food antioxidants. It contains a broad spectrum of natural, cell-protecting antioxidants, including:

- the antioxidant vitamins B_1, B_6
- the minerals zinc, manganese, and copper
- the amino acid methionine
- and the super antioxidants: beta carotene, vitamin E, Superoxide Dismutase and the trace element selenium

Spirulina is nature's richest whole-food source of gamma linolenic acid (GLA). Its oils are three times richer in GLA than evening primrose oil, a pressed oil which is not a whole food source. Spirulina is 21–29% GLA. Of all the plant sources of GLA, only spirulina provides it in a whole-food form. The only other food source of GLA is human breast milk. The body uses GLA to make a hormone-like substance called prostaglandin E1 (PGE_1) which performs a variety of functions including preventing heart attacks and strokes, slowing the production of cholesterol, improving nerve function, etc. Studies have indicated that GLA also helps reduce high blood pressure and eases such conditions as arthritis, premenstrual pain, eczema, and other skin conditions.

Spirulina is nature's richest whole-food source of chlorophyll, the key ingredient in green superfoods. With a chemical structure remarkably similar to human hemoglobin, chlorophyll helps to build the blood, renew tissues and counteract radiation. Spirulina is many times richer in chlorophyll than alfalfa or wheat grass.

Spirulina is nature's richest whole-food source of complete protein.

Spirulina	60–70%	Eggs	12–16%
Soybeans	30–35%	Tofu	8%
Beef	18–22%	Milk	3%

PURE
PLANET
PRODUCTS

4
Pure Planet® Spirulina
Shortened Typical Analysis

General Composition

Moisture	7%
Protein	60%
Lipids	6%
Carbohydrate	19%
Minerals	8%
Digestibility	95.1%

Nucleic Acids:

RNA	3.5%
DNA	1.0%

Pigments and Enzymes:
(per 10g/20 tablets/1½ Tbsp)

Phycocyanin	1110 mg
Chlorophyll	79 mg
Carotenoids	40 mg
Superoxide Dismutase	4 mg

Essential Fatty Acids:
(per 10 g/20 tablets/1½ Tbsp)

Linoleic Acid	110 mg
GLA	100 mg

Essential Amino Acids:

Isoleucine	5.43%
Leucine	8.15%
Lysine	4.37%
Methionine	2.22%
Phenylalanin	4.35%
Threonine	4.68%
Tryptophan	1.41%
Valine	6.23%

Nonessential Amino Acids:

Alanine	7.74%
Arginine	7.94%
Aspartic Acid	12.14%
Cystine	0.93%
Glutamic Acid	14.07%
Glycine	5.32%
Histidine	2.50%
Proline	4.11%
Serine	4.42%
Tyrosine	3.97%

Vitamins:
(per 10g/20 tablets/1 ½ tbsp)

Beta Carotene (pro-Vitamin A)	50,000 IU
Vitamin E (d-∂ tocopherol)	3.85 IU
Thiamin B_1	3.4 mg
Riboflavin B_2	3.3 mg
Niacin B_3	20.7 mg
Pyridoxine B_6	44 mcg
Cyanocobalamin B_{12}	22 mcg
Folic Acid	3 mcg
Biotin	3.2 mcg
Pantothenic Acid	40 mcg
Inositol	6.8 mg
Bioflavonoids	8 mg

Pure Planet® Spirulina
Shortened Typical Analysis

Minerals:
(per 10g/20 tablets/1½ tbsp)

Calcium	40 mg
Phosphorus	104 mg
Sodium	73 mg
Iron	10.6 mg
Magnesium	48 mg
Zinc	1.2 mg
Copper	10 mcg
Chromium	28 mcg
Selenium	55 mcg
Manganese	2.6 mg
Potassium	152mg

Trace Minerals: .. 5,700 mg Pure Planet Spirulina has a large and broad trace mineral base.

Pure Planet's spirulina is sweetened naturally by a complex natural sugar known as rhamnose. Rhamnose is digested easily, without the need for insulin; thus, it is safe for diabetics.

5
Spirulina & The Environment

THE REMARKABLE PROPERTIES of spirulina promote health. Spirulina is one of the paths through which we rediscover the origins of life on Earth. Descendant of the first plant life, it is the link to our most ancient and primary source of life energy. With a nutritious diet, spirulina has the power to bring the human body into balance. Even more significant in this era of global environmental and ecological concerns, spirulina has the power to heal our ailing planet.

Beginning 3 billion years ago, blue-green algae began fixing atmospheric nitrogen, converting carbon dioxide to sugars, and releasing free oxygen to eventually produce the oxygen-rich atmosphere necessary for other life to evolve. This process required over a billion years.

Since the industrial revolution—a mere grain of sand in the dunes of time—modern civilization has laid to waste much of the earth's natural resources in the name of progress. Ironically, this very progress is consuming earth's bounty much faster than it can be replenished. The inevitable outcome may be the destruction of life on Earth as we know it.

At Pure Planet® we know that spirulina—a source of life on Earth—can be the resource that helps to rejuvenate our planet Earth. Spirulina cultivation is economically sound and environmentally safe. It grows so prolifically that a cultivated area one half the size of Indiana could feed 6 ¼ billion people, which is the estimated population for the entire world in another decade.

Spirulina can be cultivated on what is now considered worthless wasteland. This would release current farmland from production to allow the land time to heal and regenerate. Much of the present farmland would, in fact, no longer be needed. Reforested farmland would help re-green the earth and check the global warming caused by the buildup of carbon dioxide in the atmosphere.

It challenges the mind that a tiny, blue-green water plant could do so much on such a vast scale. However, spirulina is only one among 25,000 species of algae, which together make up two-thirds of the total plant biomass on Earth today.

The Spirulina revolution has just begun. Each day, as more and more people discover its' health benefits, the vision of what spirulina means for the future health of ourselves and the earth becomes clearer.

Green Superfoods
Nutritional Comparison

Composition	Spirulina pacifica	Chlorella	AFA Klamath	Barley green	Wheat grass
Protein	60-70%	58%	58%	25-48%	25%
Carbohydrates	19%	23%	7%	23-40%	54%
Fats *(lipids)*	6%	9%	6%	2-5%	4%
Minerals *(ash)*	8%	5%	23%	15-25%	12%
Moisture	7%	5%	6%	5%	5%
Vitamins *(per 10 grams)*					
Beta carotene	50000 IU	5550 IU	13340 IU	5200 IU	6608 IU
Vitamin C	0.5 mg	1 mg	5 mg	33 mg	31 mg
Vitamin E	1.5 mg	0.1 IU	*	*	3 IU
B_1 *(thiamine)*	3.4 mg	0.17 mg	0.03 mg	0.13 mg	0.10 mg
B_2 *(riboflavin)*	3.3 mg	0.43 mg	0.25 mg	0.28 mg	0.20 mg
B_3 *(niacin)*	20.7 mg	2.38 mg	0.65 mg	1.06 mg	0.75 mg
B_5 *(pantothenic acid)*	40 mcg	130 mcg	*	250 mcg	240 mcg
B_6 *(pyridoxine)*	44 mcg	140 mcg	67 mcg	30 mcg	128 mcg
B_{12} *(cobalamin)*	22 mcg	13 mcg	74 mcg	*	4.3 mcg
Folic Acid	3 mcg	2.7 mcg	*	64 mcg	108 mcg
Biotin	3.2 mg	19 mcg	*	4.8 mcg	11 mcg
Inositol	6.8 mg	13.2 mg	*	*	*
Minerals *(per 10 grams)*					
Calcium	40 mg	22 mg	140 mg	111 mg	52 mg
Iron	10.6 mg	13 mg	6.4 mg	1.6 mg	5.7 mg
Magnesium	48 mg	32 mg	16 mg	22 mg	20 mg
Sodium	73 mg	0 mg	0 mg	78 mg	20 mg
Potassium	152 mg	90 mg	100 mg	888 mg	143 mg
Phosphorus	104 mg	90 mg	*	60 mg	52 mg
Zinc	1.2 mg	7 mg	0.3 mg	0.7 mg	0.5 mg
Manganese	2.6 mg	*	0.3 mg	0.6 mg	1.0 mg
Copper	10 mcg	10 mcg	60 mcg	140 mcg	140 mcg
Chromium	28 mcg	*	60 mcg	*	*
Boron	1 mg	*	*	*	*

continued overleaf

Composition	Spirulina pacifica	Chlorella	AFA Klamath	Barley green	Wheat grass
Pigments & Enzymes *(per 10 grams)*					
Phycocyanin	1110 mg	none	none	none	none
Chlorophyll	79 mg	280 mg	300 mg	149 mg	55 mg
Carotenoids	40 mg	*	*	*	*
Superoxide dismutase	(SOD) 4 mg	*	*	*	*
Fatty Acids & Lipids *(per 10 grams)*					
Gamma linolenic (GLA)	100 mg	none	*	none	none
Glycolipids	200 mg	*	*	*	*
Sulfolipids	4-10 mg	*	*	*	*

indicates no data available

6
How Does Spirulina Compare
With the Other Green Superfoods?

UTRITIONALLY MORE POTENT than regular vegetables, all the green superfoods are highly concentrated whole food sources of vitamins, minerals, amino acids, enzymes, and chlorophyll. Because they are whole foods, most are absorbed better into the bloodstream than supplements. However, not all green superfoods stack up equally when comparing the overall benefits they provide.

Of the four other foods, there are some concerns about the safety of eating Aphanizomenon flos-aquae algae (often referred to as Klamath blue-green algae or AFA). A. flos-aquae is harvested naturally from a lake and has been known to sometimes contain potent nerve toxins. Spirulina, on the other hand, is carefully grown and harvested to ensure its purity and maximize the levels of its nutrients.

Chlorella is also carefully cultivated like spirulina. However, unlike spirulina whose cell walls are easily dissolved by digestive enzymes, chlorella's cell walls are much thicker and not as easily digestible. Even when Chlorella's cell walls are cracked either chemically or mechanically, the nutrition is still not as readily available as the nutrition in spirulina. Moreover, in a recent article on the effects of spirulina on the AIDS virus, cancer, and the immune system, it reported that chlorella does not have the same anti-viral, anti-cancer and immune stimulating properties as spirulina.

Spirulina has the highest protein content and the highest amounts of beta carotene and vitamin E of all the superfoods. In addition, spirulina contains phycocyanin and other carotenoids which none of the others contain and significant amounts of gamma linolenic acid (GLA), glycolipids and sulfolipids, while the others, at best, contain only trace amounts.

All of these rare nutrients show promise as effective agents in building a strong immune system. Glycolipids extracted from spirulina have been found to combat the AIDS virus (*Boyd, et al, 1989*). Phycocyanin, the blue protein in spirulina, is demonstrating positive results with treating cancer and in stimulating the immune system (*Iijima, et al, 1982*). It stimulates the immature or damaged immune system to grow or to repair itself when injured or weakened by infection or toxic chemicals. GLA has been found to have a positive effect in the treatment of arthritis (*Belch, et al, 1988*), and premenstrual syndrome (*Horrobin, 1983*), and in protecting the body against degenerative diseases (*Kendler, 1987*).

7
Growing Process for Pure Planet® Spirulina

HE SPIRULINA PACIFICA used by Pure Planet® is a specially-bred strain of the edible microalgae Spirulina platensis. It is grown on the pristine Kona Coast of the Big Island of Hawaii adjacent to the Pacific Ocean in beautiful blue-green, open ponds approximately 30 cm deep. A combination of fresh, artesian well water and deep ocean water, drawn from a depth of 2,000 feet, is used to fill the spirulina ponds.

The other major components required for growing *Spirulina pacifica* are food-grade baking soda (sodium bicarbonate) and carbon dioxide. Ninety-six trace elements are supplied by the deep sea water. Paddle wheels agitate the water, ensuring even exposure of the algae to the sun. The culture thrives in these ideal conditions, growing several times faster than it does in the wild.

This species of *Spirulina pacifica* developed by aquaculturists is uniquely nutritious and potent and has several times the natural beta carotene of wild strains of blue-green algae. The cultivated ponds are tested and sampled every day ensuring the consumer a pure product. *Spirulina pacifica* is pumped from the culture ponds through underground pipes to a building where it is screened for grit and then separated from the culture medium by stainless steel screens. It is then washed three times with fresh water, vacuum filtered, and spray dried by the Ocean-Chill system.

Within minutes of harvest, the spirulina paste is fed into a dryer. A great deal of research has gone into which method of drying protects the nutrient quality of the spirulina during the drying process. The Ocean-Chill system of modified spray drying, developed by scientists in Hawaii, eliminates oxygen from the dryer, increasing retention of beta carotene and enzyme activity. The spirulina dries in three seconds and is immediately packaged. Although heat is used in the drying process, the spirulina is kept at temperatures low enough to preserve the vital enzymes of this delicate blue-green algae.

Spirulina pacifica is certified free of pesticides and herbicides and certified Kosher. The processing facilities are certified for food production and are operated under Good Manufacturing Practices (GMP) and ISO 9000. They are inspected by the U.S. Food & Drug Administration (FDA) and the Hawaii State Department of Health.

8
Building Our Immune
System with Pure Planet® Spirulina

UR IMMUNE SYSTEM plays a central role in our optimal health and disease prevention. It is the
immune system that produces the blood's white
cells—the white knights in our body—and other
faithful protectors against all manner of foreign substances
that cripple our systems and may eventually cause disease
and death.

Composed of a complex network of proteins, organs, glands
and cells, the immune system's primary function is to neu-
tralize or remove any infectious organisms or foreign bodies.
In an extremely involved process, the white blood cells sense
invading foreign cells and secrete chemicals that surround and
destroy the invaders. The most active of these white blood cells
are called T-cells and B-cells. We need active T- and B-cells to
protect ourselves during every breathing moment because the
body is continuously being bombarded by innumerable toxins
in the environment. These include polluted air, viruses, infectious diseases, pollen and toxic bacteria.

The antibodies fashioned by the T- and B-cells are known
as immunoglobulins. The immunoglobulins in our system
decrease whenever the T- and B-cells are eliminated by an especially potent group of invaders. This makes us vulnerable to
further invasion. The AIDS virus, for example, virtually eliminates all the T-cells. With the immune system no longer functioning properly, the infected person becomes particularly vulnerable to a great variety of other diseases, which may
ultimately cause death. Spirulina is showing itself to be an
incredible immune system ally. It can help us strengthen our
T- and B-cells as well as the rest of our immune system.

Nutrition and the Immune System

HIPPOCRATES ONCE SAID, "Let food be your medicine." This sage advice is especially relevant today, when so many diseases have been found to be diet related. For example, research has shown that approximately 35% of all deaths from cancer are directly related to diet (*Doll & Peto 1981*). It is estimated that 40% of cancer among men and 60% of cancer among women is dietary related (*Wynder & Cori 1979*).

The basic principle of nutrition is that all nutrients should work synergistically with each other. The interactions among the nutrients, not just their individual qualities, form the basis of healthy biological functioning. This synergistic requirement has been overlooked in this pill-popping age. It's also the reason why many of the medical studies done on single nutrients have been failures.

Spirulina is an ideal food source. With its natural, non-synthetic spectrum of vitamins, minerals, amino acids, trace elements, essential fatty acids and pigments, spirulina builds the body's immune system. Moreover, given its remarkable absorbability within the bloodstream, spirulina delivers optimum nutrition where it counts, at the cellular level.

Recent research conducted with spirulina on the AIDS virus indicates astonishing results. In 1996, scientists performing ongoing research at the Dana-Farber Cancer Institute, Harvard Medical School and Earthrise Farms found that small concentrations of a spirulina extract decreased the HIV-1 viral replication in cells and larger concentrations actually stopped the replication of the viral cells altogether. Elsewhere, other in-vitro studies with a purified water extract of spirulina demonstrated the same inhibiting effect on viral cell replication with a variety of other infections including herpes simplex, Influenza A, and mumps and measles viruses.

Key Nutrients in Rebuilding and Strengthening the Immune System

LET'S LOOK AT HOW some of these key nutrients enhance the function of a healthy immune system:

Beta carotene is a vitally important antioxidant. It is especially newsworthy due to its success in helping many cancer patients. A Harvard University research team is studying the effects of naturally occurring beta carotene in the inhibition and regression of cancer. The objective of the research is to determine how beta carotene affects the immune system and triggers the body's natural defense mechanisms, the recruitment and stimulation of macrophages, the production of tumor necrosis factor (TNF), and possibly other immune-system modifiers.

So far, results of the research at Harvard show that beta carotene causes the inhibition and regression of cancer in animals and in cultured human and animal cancer cells. In some of the experiments, beta carotene extracted from spirulina was more effective than synthetic beta carotene in killing cultured cancer cells. These results suggest that beta carotene derived from spirulina products works, at least in part, by triggering the body's own immune system defense mechanisms.

Beta carotene is most commonly found naturally in fruits and vegetables. However, The National Research Council and other research organizations recommend daily amounts of servings of these foods which easily exceed most people's daily intake. Spirulina contains the highest amount of beta carotene to be found in a whole food source. With all of the other immune enhancing nutrients contained in it as well, what better choice can be made for a beta carotene source?

Vitamin E is believed to have the ability to destroy free radicals because of its antioxidant properties. Vitamin E bolsters the production of antibodies. Its deficiency lowers levels of antibodies, as well as the crucial T- and B-cells. Studies show that vitamin E increases stamina and helps build up resistance to degenerative diseases such as arthritis. Spirulina, nature's richest whole food source of vitamin E, supplies three times more vitamin E than raw wheat germ. The berry-flavored Super-Natural Meal™, with its whole freeze-dried berries, doubles the amount of vitamin E.

Selenium and zinc are major players in a robust immune system and can also be found in spirulina. Selenium works synergistically with vitamin E as an antioxidant. A deficiency in this mineral causes a drop in the B-cell response, resulting in lower levels of antibodies. Zinc is critical to the immune system because it is an essential co-factor in more than 100 enzymes. A zinc deficiency leads to low levels of blood immunoglobulins and increases the body's susceptibility to infections.

Spirulina also contains many rare and unique nutrients not found in other foods. One of these is phycocyanin, a blue protein structurally similar to erythropoietin (EPO), the growth hormone that regulates bone marrow cells producing blood cells. Phycocyanin greatly enhances the action of the immune system, protecting the body from degenerative diseases. Another unique nutrient is gamma linolenic acid (GLA), found only in the seeds of a few flowers, human breast milk, and spirulina. GLA stimulates the production of prostaglandins which regulate growth and function of the heart, blood and musculature. GLA is critically important to cell function. Research has shown that cells deficient in GLA are fragile and have diminished growth, loss of tone, impaired water balance and a variety of degenerative changes, all of which can impair functioning of the immune system.

B vitamins are also valued members of the immune system team:

B₂ (riboflavin), which keeps the mucosal lining of the body healthy, is one of the first defense barriers against disease.

B3 (niacin), stimulates circulation and is important to the nervous system and brain. The coenzymes in niacin help the body to utilize proteins, fats and carbohydrates

B6 (pyridoxine) produces nucleic acid and protein. When B6 is deficient, the thymus gland, a crucial part of the immune system, shrinks.

B_{12} and folic acid are both needed by the immune system cells. The bone marrow and the thymolymphatic organs are the home base for the immune system cells. The T- and B-cells are produced in the bone marrow to mature into active disease fighters. A deficiency in either B_{12} or folic acid causes a decrease in T- and B-cells and shrinking of the thymolymphatic organs.

Spirulina contains all of these important B vitamins. Although vitamin B_{12} is the most difficult of all vitamins to obtain from vegetable sources, spirulina is extremely rich in this vitamin. The SuperNatural Meal™, with its additional sprouted barley and grains, provides up to 404% of vitamin B_{12} in addition to providing higher quantities of some of the other B vitamins and folic acid.

The extensive and beneficial effects of vitamin C are well known. Vitamin C, essential for tissue growth and repair and adrenal gland function, protects against infection and the harmful effects of pollution, enhances the immune system, and helps the body resist cancer. Studies show that antioxidants also help muscles recover and regenerate more quickly following exercise. Recent research has uncovered further benefits of vitamin C in the fight against cholesterol, diabetes, high blood pressure, cataracts, male infertility, stress, and possibly AIDS.

Vitamin C plays a major, intricate role in the body's complex immune system. It controls the production of T-lymphocytes (T-cells), increases the antibody levels and increases the production of interferon, proteins with anti-viral activity. An amazing antioxidant, vitamin C neutralizes harmful oxidants and free radicals and keeps the mineral portion of certain enzymes in their proper reduced state. Vitamin C has anti-inflammatory properties as well. It inhibits the production of certain hormones which are involved in tissue inflammation and the accompanying swelling, pain, tenderness and heat. Studies suggest that regular vitamin C intake may alleviate the pain and stiffness of arthritis.

Vitamin C is also essential in the metabolism of other nutrients needed by the body, like folic acid, tyrosine and phenylalanine, and it is essential in the formation of collagen, the connective protein which binds tissue together.

Vitamin C has a beneficial effect on the immune system and should be part of everyone's dietary regimen. Because vitamin C is the only one of these key nutrients found in relatively small amounts in spirulina, several of our products contain a superior form of vitamin C, Ester-C®. (See page 28 for more details.)

Amino acids play an integral role in the immune system as well. Both the essential and nonessential amino acids must be present for protein synthesis to occur. The role of proteins in rebuilding cells and repairing tissue is well understood, and proteins do much more, especially in strengthening and supporting the immune system. Proteins form antibodies to combat invading bacteria and viruses. Proteins also build nucleoproteins such as RNA and DNA, which assist in moving oxygen through the body and play a major role in muscle activity. Proteins need to be available constantly since they are in a dynamic state, being continuously utilized and re-synthesized. Simply stated, our body needs proteins and proteins need amino acids.

Iron deficiency has been linked to a wide variety of defects in immune response functions. Ten grams of spirulina contain 10 mg of iron, more iron than a regular serving of either spinach or beef liver. In fact, a diet supplemented with spirulina shows a 60% higher absorption of iron because spirulina is a rich whole-food source of biochelated organic iron. A high iron bio-availability is documented to have a related effect in the correction of anemia.

Ultimately, we are responsible for our own health and there are some preventive measures we must take for our own benefit. Studies show that, along with appropriate diet and superfoods, we can help build our immune system response by abstaining from stimulants and drugs, performing regular exercise, avoiding overexposure to the sun, eating sensibly and honoring and expressing our emotions. Our own best efforts will go a long way toward maintaining a strong, healthy immune system.

Health and wholeness are becoming more and more a necessity, not a choice, in this day and age. Pure Planet® superfoods have a major, natural role in this life philosophy.

9
Spirulina for Athletes
& Bodybuilders

N ATHLETE TRAINS hard, makes great progress, and then it strikes: No more gains. That record time, distance, or poundage continues to be elusive.To get through this barrier and resume the climb to higher peaks of performance, the athlete needs a better understanding of the engine of life, the human cell.

Every living thing is composed of cells and life is based on a vast continuous series of electrochemical changes that take place in and around them. Intense training places incredible stress on the ability of the cells to adapt to the desired level of growth and energy production.

In skeletal muscle, individual cells (called fibers) can be up to 30 centimeters in length. Bundles of these fibers, known as motor units, may contain anywhere from five muscle fibers to two thousand. Acting like cables, contractions of these motor units pull bones and produce movement. As the contractions become faster and stronger, so do the body's movements.

Reaching a plateau where no further gains are being made means that the motor unit's adaptive response has reached its limit. To keep pushing it will either cause nothing to happen or catastrophe could strike and the engine will blow. The adaptive response or level of functional output is directly related to the level of metabolism or energy production within the cells. To raise the adaptive response and start making gains again, better metabolism is required to promote stronger contractions and increase growth of contractive protein chains within the muscle fiber. This requires high quality nutrition.

The food consumed must nourish more than muscle cells because the cells comprise only 35–45% of the body's weight. There are many other cells which compete for every ounce of nutrition. Every minute, some three hundred million cells or more wear out and die in the body, most of them replaced immediately by division of the cells that remain. Intense training increases the amount of cell destruction and places extra demands on available nutrients for recovery and repair. If the food one consumes is not supplying sufficient nutrition to meet this extra demand, muscle fibers are forced to operate partially starved and further gains and progress are impossible.

Almost everyone in training has made some effort toward improving their nutrition. Supplementation can provide many benefits for the body builder, however, it may be difficult to sort out what is right given the abundance of products on the market today. Vitamin and mineral tablets, protein drinks, and expensive free-form amino acids are standard purchases in the sports industry. A great deal of money could be spent on these with no guarantee of positive results. Often, one of two things will happen: either the product does not work, or the athlete may not be using enough of it. A good way to get back on track is to return to nutritional basics with plenty of whole, unprocessed, unrefined food.

Calories are essential to support growth, repair, and energy production. It is impossible to build muscle mass while consuming fewer calories than are required to meet current energy demands. This is problematic for runners who are trying to stay lean but still retain muscle. Insufficient intake of calories forces the body to start breaking down muscle, and it is quite common to see runners who become emaciated in chest and facial muscles because of this. A good nutritional basis for building mass requires vitamins, minerals, high quality complete protein, complex carbohydrates, plenty of water, and a little bit of dietary unsaturated fat.

With basic building blocks established and in place, one can then look at the supplements which will most enhance a nutritional program. This is an important choice which will make the difference to each individual for reaching maximum potential and performance. Some say that complete nutrition can be obtained from a well balanced basic diet. That was true in another age when soils were rich with minerals and only fresh, unprocessed foods were consumed. Now, however, it is important that athletes and bodybuilders have concentrated sources of whole-food nutrition.

The most consistently successful supplements are generally the most natural ones. Food yeast is a good example, giving a great boost to the metabolism with its rich supply of B vitamins and protein. The superstar, however, is spirulina. *Spirulina pacifica* contains 65% complete protein, with all of the essential amino acids including the Branched Chain Amino Acids (BCAA's) for muscle biosynthesis and arginine.

Because spirulina's cell walls are made of complex sugars, its nutrients are easily and quickly absorbed. Rapid absorption is the key to strong muscular performance. And, unlike denatured, highly processed protein powders which are difficult to absorb, spirulina is natural, with its nutrients in a biologically active form the body can instantly utilize. Within seconds, the concentrated nutrients and enzymes in spirulina are absorbed into the bloodstream. No other food can provide as much nutrition so quickly. This is why most athletes speak of the energy boost they get when taking spirulina.

The gamma linolenic acid (GLA) contained in spirulina is also important to athletic performance. Research has shown that cells deficient in GLA are fragile, with diminished growth, loss of tone, impaired water balance and a variety of degenerative changes, all of which can impair training for maximum performance. A rare nutrient, GLA is found only in the seeds of a few flowers, human breast milk and spirulina!

Many athletes take ten or more spirulina tablets with water 30 minutes before training. While working out blood engorges around the muscles and concentrates the nutrients where they are needed during peak stress periods. The SuperNatural Meal™, with its ten grams of spirulina and ten grams of organic sprouted barley, provides liquid calories with enzymes and naturally biochelated minerals and amino acids. This combination allows for optimal utilization of the protein for muscle growth.

Power Carob-Mint Spirulina™ gave Kawika Spaulding of Hawaii his edge in the 1994 MoonBat Trans America Footrace and the 1997 Malama I Ka Aina Aloha O Hawaii race around the island of Hawaii. In the 1994 MoonBat race, five out of fourteen runners completed the grueling 64-day, 3000-mile marathon from Los Angeles to New York City. Forty year old Kawika Spaulding ate fifty to sixty Carob-Mint Spirulina tablets daily as he ran across America and stunned everyone by finishing after so many others were forced to drop out. Kawika depended on this amazing power food on days when he couldn't eat anything else. In the 1997 Hawaii race, fueled by Power Carob-Mint Spirulina™ again, Kawika Spaulding took first place, running 228 miles in four days.

Power Carob-Mint Spirulina™ powered former mountain guide Dan Stocking of Juneau, Alaska when he and his teammates made their June, 1995 attempt on the highest peak in North America: 20,320-foot Denali/Mt. McKinley in Denali National Park. Dan has been a mountain climber and spirulina consumer for over ten years and for this climb chose Pure Planet® Power Carob-Mint Spirulina™ for its excellent nutritional and energy-boosting qualities. Eating thirty to sixty tablets daily, Dan later wrote that he felt better at high altitude on this climb than on many others, even after a night in an ice cave at 16,200 feet and carrying a one hundred-pound pack: "I felt good and strong and I know that your Power Carob-Mint Spirulina™ played a major role in my endurance."

Providing everything the body needs for complete metabolism, spirulina acts like an high octane booster for the fuel in the cellular engine. This in turn increases one's level of adaptive response for optimal and healthy performance. Great gains can be made and one's overall level of fitness increased.

Many athletes see noticeable improvements in performance within a few weeks. Try it and see why Olympic and world champion athletes depend on spirulina everyday.

10
Slimming with Spirulina

OSING WEIGHT, or more specifically, body fat can be a source of frustration to those changing their eating habits. This is largely due to a lack of knowledge about body chemistry, and the various ways the body stores and uses nutrition, especially as it relates to the accumulation, use and storage of fat.

Though decreasing food intake may lower overall weight, cutting calories alone does not maintain muscle tissue nor does it reverse the altered chemistry of the muscles, nor does it permanently keep the body from resuming its previous fat set point. In fact, a weight loss quick-fix attacks subcutaneous fat first and will remove intramuscular fat only under the most severe circumstances. To instruct the body to undergo such rigor would be disappointing at best because nothing prevents weight gain once again. Radical dieting, unbalanced eating, shots and fasting can worsen the situation because they have been shown to lessen muscle mass as the person is losing fat.

How does the body respond to all of this? The body's first reaction is to draw on the energy that is immediately available in any emergency. This is not fat; the body has no means to make immediate use of stored fat. The body's immediately available form of energy is a substance called glycogen which is a form of glucose (a carbohydrate) stored with water in the muscles and in the body's most metabolically active vital organ, the liver.

For many years it was assumed that the glycogen stored in the liver was the principal source of blood sugar between meals. However, more recently it has been shown that this glycogen is hoarded by the liver. Instead of giving up its glycogen for blood sugar, the liver converts protein to glucose. This means that if the body were to subsist on a starvation diet, it would actually convert valuable body protein to blood sugar as fuel for the brain.

Spirulina is the only plant food that contains glycogen. Glycogen is not ordinarily available through our diet. Muscles store glycogen and use it as a principal source of both immediate and long-term energy. The more glycogen available during intense or sustained exercise, the greater the potential for improved functioning. When glycogen levels drop, weakness and fatigue set in rapidly. Spirulina shortcuts the metabolic process of synthesizing glycogen from our food and supplies it directly pre-formed, thus sparing the body's own glycogen reserves.

The amount of fat that we might gain is not genetically pre-ordained, but determined by our chosen lifestyles. When a person reaches adult weight, the body establishes the enzyme system, hormone levels, and musculoskeletal pattern to remain at that weight. Whatever amount of fat one maintains for a period of a year or more then becomes the body's reference point. From then on all body systems will be geared to that reference or fat set point. The body protects its fat cells against invasion and deprivation just as it protects all other cells, so if overweight for a year or more, the body demands to be kept at this set point.

Exercise is a key component which can successfully help reset the body's set point. Daily exercise, such as aerobic, brisk walking, where the lungs are breathing deeply and the heart is working vigorously, forms a central part of permanent fat-loss. This is true for two major reasons: first, regular aerobic exercise stimulates metabolism which in itself helps burn fat and, second, such exercise encourages the rapid and efficient elimination of toxicity from the system through the breath, the skin (in the form of sweat), the bowels and the kidneys. It even improves the functions of the liver which is absolutely central to solving the problem of excess fat-stores in the body.

Although results differ slightly from one study to another, the general consensus is that one needs to exercise aerobically at least four times a week, for at least thirty to forty uninterrupted minutes at each session. Frequency of exercise matters greatly. Those who exercise four or five times a week tend to lose weight two to three times faster than those who exercise only three times a week. Fewer than three sessions a week are shown to be completely ineffective in weight loss. Some of the best forms of aerobic exercise are: rapid and vigorous walking, steady jogging or running, swimming, biking or cross-country skiing.

It is important when exercising to maintain your own reasonable level of exertion. Exercising too hard for your individual body is dangerous, and is ineffectual for encouraging fat-burning. Under too much strain, muscles switch to an anaerobic method of extracting energy. This increases toxicity in the body and interferes with the desired oxidation of stored fat.

A key factor to explain why some people lose weight while some seem to maintain normal weight effortlessly is the efficiency of special tissue in the back of the neck and along the spine, called brown adipose tissue or brown fat. Unlike ordinary yellow fat, brown fat has a very high metabolic response to any excess calories consumed by burning them off as body heat rather than storing them as fat. Unfortunately, many overweight people suffer from under-active brown fat.

A number of factors are known to contribute to the activation of brown fat. Interestingly, the essential fatty acid (EFA) content of body fat is inversely proportional to body weight. This means that the higher the level of EFA's in the body, the lower the body weight, and vice versa.

At the University of Wales in Cardiff, studies indicate that gamma linoleic acid (GLA) has a stimulating effect on brown fat tissue. The prostaglandins, which are the end products of GLA metabolism, possibly accelerate the mitochondria activity of the brown fat. There is no readily available better food source of GLA than spirulina.

Spirulina also contains phenylalanine which is a natural appetite suppressant. Phenylalanine, an amino acid, produces a chemical known as cholecystokinin which, in turn, acts quickly on the appetite center of the hypothalamus in the brain. This helps suppress appetite. Spirulina is one of the most easily assimilated forms of protein which keeps blood sugar at the correct level and prevents hunger pangs. Taking six to ten tablets of 100% Pure Spirulina™ on an empty stomach one half hour before meals is an effective and beneficial method for weight loss.

Spirulina is an exceptionally rich source of arginine, an amino acid that releases growth hormone (Gh). Gh is a polypeptide hormone that is secreted by the pituitary gland. Gh stimulates the body's own regenerative process by increasing the rate of protein synthesis. It causes muscle cells to grow and multiply by directly increasing the rate at which amino acids enter the muscles and are built up into protein. Gh promotes fat burning, causing cells to switch from burning carbohydrates to burning fat for energy. It stimulates fat tissues to release stored fat and it stimulates other cells to break down the released fat molecules.

Teenagers with their high levels of Gh can generally eat thousands of calories and not become overweight. In contrast, a middle-aged person eating the same food and getting the same amount of exercise with substantially less Gh will likely put on additional fat.

With a desire to decrease body fat, one must increase lean muscle tissue and muscle enzymes through exercising and ensuring that the diet contains branched chain amino acids (BCAA's) for muscle biosynthesis. Three BCAA's, leucine, isoleucine and valine, provide more than 70% of all the free nitrogen to the body and regulate muscle protein synthesis. Even if one is sedentary, 90% of all the calories burned are burned by the muscles. Specialized enzymes existing only in muscle tissue can increase fat burning by fifty-fold during exercise. Eating the three BCAA's will supply fuel and be converted into glucose for energy when you have high energy demands and diminishing blood sugar levels. If dietary BCAA's are lacking, the body will break down its own muscle tissue resulting in loss of lean muscle mass, lowered metabolism and increased fat deposition.

Spirulina is nature's richest source of BCAA's. It is important to eat as much live or biogenic food as possible. The word biogenic means life-generating, and it refers to living, enzyme-rich, raw foods. Living foods have special properties for both weight-loss and high-level health. Fresh fruits (organic whenever possible), sprouted seeds, and grains have the highest complement of vitamins and minerals, essential fatty acids, easily assimilated top quality protein, fiber and wholesome carbohydrates. Such a natural complement of nutrients in superbly balanced form supplies the body with substances it needs to function at a high level of efficiency. This is what one wants in order to encourage steady and permanent fat loss.

Discovering spirulina and learning how to use it can awaken a deeper interest in a more natural diet through its powerful rejuvenating effects. Its supernutrition satisfies hunger because it completely meets the body's biochemical needs.

The use of spirulina can help re-establish normal sodium/potassium and acid/alkaline balance. Excess fat and water are reduced, returning the body to a leaner, better balance. The change is gentle, indirect and stable. Old habits are broken not by self-coercion, but by attraction to new habits that give an awakened sense of aliveness. This long-term subtle approach along with regular exercise and appropriate supplementation enables one to successfully stay lean and healthy.

II
Spirulina and Pregnancy

OUND NUTRITION is important for good health and especially during pregnancy. Nutrition is equally important for the expecting mother and the developing child. Since healthy mothers have healthy babies, the best thing a pregnant mother can do for her unborn infant is to make certain that the child is being continually supplied with sufficient nutrients.

The foods that a prospective mother selects (or neglects) will determine the physical and mental potential of the person growing within her. In fact, throughout the critical growth years, a baby's cellular replication rate is nothing short of phenomenal. Their nutritional needs will never be greater and deficiencies at this time can result in serious and oftentimes permanent damage.

This most critical formative environment of the child is almost entirely dependent upon the nutrients supplied by the mother's bloodstream. It is a great responsibility and tragically, oftentimes, one that is met with minimal education and guidance.

It is important to realize that a baby will take whatever she/he needs from the mother's body, often at a cost to the mother, dangerously depleting her of calcium, other minerals and vitamins. This can result in difficult labor, premature birth, or may affect her ability to nurse. The baby can simply take what nutrients are available; if a mother-to-be is deficient in nutrients, the child loses out in nutrients.

Mounting evidence, including an extensive study done recently by Professor Bryce-Smith in Britain, shows that behavioral disorders and impaired development can be linked to diet factors during fetal life. The major stages in the embryo's development occur during the first few weeks of life, before most women even know they are pregnant. Because of this, it is wise for women contemplating motherhood to consider the advantages of improving their nutrition before conception.

Iron deficiency anemia in pregnant mothers and their developing children is the number one most prevalent nutritional disorder. If undiscovered or otherwise unchecked, iron deficiency in advanced stages results in irreversible brain damage, among other things.

Iron supplements in health food stores and supermarkets abound, but most are formulations of inorganic (from non-living rock or metallic sources) iron compounds, which have markedly poor biological availability. They often cause unpleasant side effects such as lack of appetite, stomach pain, heartburn, nausea, vomiting, diarrhea and constipation. In contrast, studies have shown that the organic biochelated iron in spirulina is exceptionally well absorbed and utilized by the human body, and it is completely non-toxic. In fact, spirulina supplies 58 times more iron than raw spinach and 28 times more than raw beef liver.

Pregnant women should increase their daily amount of calcium by about 0.4g. This means that the total daily intake, especially during the last half of pregnancy, should be about 1.2g. This is a 50% increase (regular intake is 0.8g). Calcium is needed for the construction and growth of bones as well as tooth buds in the developing fetus. It is an important constituent of the blood-clotting mechanism and is also used in normal muscle action and other essential metabolic activities. Additional calcium is also critical for the rapid mineralization of skeletal tissue during the final period of growth.

Although spirulina is not known as a calcium source, it supplies more calcium, gram for gram, than virtually any other food. Only ten grams supply 14% of the recommended USRDA.

The period of gestation is an exceedingly rapid growth period. A human life grows from a single fertilized egg cell to a fully developed infant weighing about seven pounds. Such a rapid growth period places a crucial demand for increased amounts of protein in the mother's diet. Increased amounts of dietary protein are also needed for development of the placenta, enlargement of maternal tissues, increasing maternal circulating blood volume, formation of amniotic fluid and increasing storage reserves.

There seems to be consensus that pregnant and nursing mothers have a clear need for increased dietary intake of protein, yet they need it without an increase in fats and calories. A typical pregnant woman is advised to increase her protein intake from forty-four grams to seventy-four grams (68% increase) while increasing calories from 2,000 to 2,300 (15% increase). So, additional protein must be low in calories to avoid an unnecessary weight increase. Again, spirulina with its 60–70% complete high-biological value protein is an excellent choice. Animal proteins are not as good a choice for pregnant women because of their high levels of saturated fats and cholesterol, and their high residues of toxic pesticides, herbicides, drugs and hormones. Spirulina contains no poisons or toxic chemical residues.

Water retention is also a concern for pregnant women. Spirulina is also low in sodium.

A 25% increase of vitamin A (beta carotene) during pregnancy is recommended for the increased cell growth and development of the fetus, maintenance of epithelial tissue in the developing skin and internal mucosal tissues lining body cavities, tooth formation, normal bone growth and vision development. Spirulina, nature's richest whole food source of beta carotene (pro-Vitamin A), supplies more beta carotene than raw carrots. And, unlike preformed vitamin A which has been shown to cause toxicity in humans when taken in high doses, the body will convert beta carotene into only as much vitamin A as it needs. Therefore the beta carotene in spirulina is completely non-toxic even in larger doses.

During pregnancy there is also an increased need for B vitamins. These are usually supplied by the general increases indicated in the overall diet. B vitamins are important as co-enzyme factors in a number of metabolic activities, especially energy production and in muscle and nerve tissue function. Therefore these vitamins, particularly B_{12} and folic acid, play key roles in increased metabolic activities of pregnancy. Also, studies show that large proportions of post-partum psychoses may be related to a deficiency of vitamin B_{12} and folic acid. Fifteen tablets of spirulina supplies more vitamin B_{12} than a serving of fish or eggs. The SuperNatural Meal™, with its sprouted barley and additional grains, provides increased amounts of all the B vitamins and folic acid. In fact, one serving provides up to 404% of the RDA of vitamin B_{12}.

The vitamin B_{12} in spirulina is of particular interest to vegetarians since it is the most potent and reliable source of vitamin B_{12} in the vegetable kingdom. A baby fed only breast milk from his/her vegan mother can develop symptoms of pernicious anemia, a disease resulting from a lack of vitamin $B_{1}2$. The nursing mother may show no symptoms of B_{12} deficiency; she has enough of this nutrient for her own needs, but not enough to provide for the baby's needs in her milk.

Energy loss and fatigue may be commonly associated with pregnancy, especially during the first trimester. Few people are aware of how much energy our bodies spend on the intensive work of digestion. In fact, more energy is spent on digestion than on any other bodily function. It actually exceeds the amount of energy consumed during strenuous exercise. Spirulina's provision of absorbable nutrients may be of particular importance to pregnant women who are hypoglycemic, or prone to fainting, since no other food provides so much nutrition as quickly.

Since every woman is biochemically unique with different life and diet styles, they each have different nutritional needs. There is no single food or supplement that will supply (in adequate amounts) the total spectrum of nutrients required for optimal health during pregnancy other than spirulina. It is essential to eat a high-potency, low-fat diet focused principally on fresh, organic raw fruits and vegetables with sprouted grains, nuts and seeds, and complete avoidance of all processed and devitalized "foodless" foods. Spirulina, containing more than 100 synergistic nutrients, is incontestably the richest and most complete source of total organic nutrition in the world.

This educational information about spirulina and pregnancy is not intended as medical advice or as a guide for self-treatment nor is it intended to substitute for any treatment prescribed by a health practitioner. Pregnant women should consult a health professional when using spirulina or any other supplements.

12
Spirulina and Children

IMPORTANT INFORMATION regarding the use of spirulina in children's nutrition has come from controlled studies in Russia. In one such study, spirulina was used as a treatment for children contaminated by radiation from the Chernobyl disaster. These children were found to have elevated levels of immunoglobulin E (IgE) indicating high allergy sensitivity. Thirty-five children were given five grams of spirulina daily. Their IgE levels were lowered and they had less radiation sickness and fewer allergies than children in the other control group.

Regular use of spirulina in children's diets can help to modulate their consumption of junk food. Spirulina can also have positive effects on children afflicted with attention deficit disorder (ADD) as studies show that nutrition (i.e., protein consumption and minimizing sugar) can ameliorate this condition.

As with developing fetuses, children grow rapidly and require good nutrition to build better bodies.

13
Spirulina and Animals

A S BENEFICIAL as spirulina is for people, it is equally so for animals. Adding spirulina to your pet's daily diet can turn thin, dull coats into thick, healthy coats. Spirulina can nourish arthritic joints in pets and improve energy and vitality. In fact, most benefits ascribed to people are equally applicable to animals.

One interesting example of spirulina's positive effects for mammals is illustrated by the dramatic recovery of an older dolphin in a research facility in the Florida Keys. The dolphin had liver and skin disease and had lost 100 pounds from not eating. He had violent spasms of vomiting. In fact, he was dying. Dr. Christopher Lee, a spirulina expert, was visiting the facility with a friend and, upon seeing the dolphin, suggested that he be given spirulina powder. The curator of the facility agreed to try it under a controlled experiment, starting with one-eighth cup per day, working up to one-half cup daily. The dolphin began to eat again after the very first serving of spirulina and within two weeks of continued supplementation, he was well on his way to complete recovery.

Spirulina also improves the healthy color of fish as well as the texture and color of birds' plumage and plant foliage.

14
Products

Pure Planet® 100% Pure Spirulina™
World's Only 100% Pure Tablet

URE PLANET™ has perfected a method of producing the world's first and only 100% pure spirulina tablet. Unlike other manufacturers, Pure Planet® does not use binders, fillers, the granulation method, or tableting aids in their 100% pure spirulina tablets.

Tableting aids create a harder tablet that is more difficult to digest and often passes through the body undissolved. The granulation method destroys spirulina's nutritional potency. Instead, Pure Planet® uses a unique method which creates soft tablets and preserves all of the nutritional potency by allowing only minimal exposure to light, moisture, heat and oxygen. Pure Planet Products® guarantees the best-tasting, purest and freshest tablets and powders.

Spirulina properly sealed in air-tight, dark brown glass or plastic bottles will have a shelf life of two to three years. Further shelf life can be obtained from packaging in vacumn sealed, oxygen/light-barrier bags; ideal for long-term storage and emergency preparedness.

Because of spirulina's superior long term shelf life and balanced nutritional profile, spirulina is an excellent whole food for emergency preparedness. Spirulina has the additional advantage of being both lightweight and compact to store.

Pure Planet® Power Carob-Mint Spirulina™

PURE PLANET® Power Carob-Mint Spirulina™ tastes delicious and refreshing and provides instant energy. It is highly nutritious and safe to take even in large doses. Power Carob-Mint Spirulina™ provides an energy boost for people on the go. For the physically active—both regular and occasional athletes—

Power Carob-Mint Spirulina™ can make exercise healthier. It provides easily absorbable nutrition which is needed for sustained physical activity. For the athlete who burns energy faster and is more susceptible to tissue injury through physical stress, the nutritional power of spirulina is fortified with Ester-C® and L-glycine, both well-known for their beneficial effects on the human body. Researchers claim the antioxidant vitamins C and E strengthen resistance to injury and promote muscle recovery and regeneration. Power Carob-Mint Spirulina™ is the ultimate energizer for the physically active.

Power Ingredients:

PURE SPIRULINA: Pure Planet® Spirulina is the main ingredient in Power Carob-Mint Spirulina™. Spirulina contains all of the nutrients the body needs and, being so highly absorbable, makes spirulina a natural energy food.

Ester-C® is a superior form of vitamin C. It is non-acidic and highly absorbable. Vitamin C metabolites are the key differences between Ester-C® ascorbate and other vitamin C products. It contains naturally bonded minerals that allow entry to the blood cells and provide nutrition to the body.

Glycine: L-glycine is a simple amino acid that is needed for synthesizing nonessential amino acids. It is required for central nervous system function and contributes to improved blood circulation, and healthy pituitary and prostate glands. Glycine helps retard muscle degeneration by supplying additional creatine, which is normally formed in the muscle and is essential for muscle function. It also releases energy to be used by muscles, stabilizes blood sugar and mobilizes fat.

Carob: With a flavor similar to chocolate, carob is a nutritionally superior alternative. Unlike chocolate, carob is low in fat and calories and contains no acids, caffeine or other stimulants. It is naturally sweet; it is an excellent source of protein, carbohydrate, phosphorus, potassium, calcium, iron, pectin and vitamins A, B_1 (thiamin) and B_3 (niacin); and, it is nonaddictive and virtually non-allergenic.

Mint Powder: The refreshing mint flavor will leave breath cool and fresh...

Pure, Natural and Healthy

PURE PLANET® Power Carob-Mint Spirulina™ is available in powder and tablet form. It can be taken alone or with other foods and is an ideal snack for the health-conscious. Only the purest ingredients are used: no chocolate, sugar, animal/dairy products, oils or synthetic additives. Power Carob-Mint Spirulina™ tastes good and is nutritious.

There are many ways to enjoy Power Carob-Mint Spirulina™. Here are some suggestions:

- Have a Power Carob-Mint Spirulina™ drink before physical activity; or take Power tabs for melt-in-the-mouth nutrition during workouts or trainings. It is easily transportable for long runs.
- Pack Power Carob-Mint Spirulina™ tablets in a backpack or pocket and eat them while enjoying a hike or bike ride: no dealing with messy wrappers.
- Blend Power Carob-Mint Spirulina™ with soy or rice milk to make a delicious, creamy shake. Top off with a scoop of non-dairy ice cream.
- Add Power Carob-Mint Spirulina™ to a favorite cookie or brownie recipe for extra flavor and nutrition. Reserve some batter and mix in Power Carob-Mint Spirulina™ to create a wonderful swirl for a cake.
- Add Power Carob-Mint Spirulina™ to a tapioca, pudding or custard recipe.

Power Carob-Mint Spirulina™ is the natural choice over energy bars, sugar-filled green drinks and synthetic supplements. Indulge your sweet tooth and get complete nutrition at the same time.

Ester-C® PLUS™ — The Ultimate Vitamin C

Ester-C® PLUS™ is a unique, powerful combination of Ester-C® and Pure Planet® Spirulina. The individual components of Ester-C® (containing metabolites) and spirulina (containing bioflavonoids and biocarotenoids) work synergistically to enhance each other's absorption into the bloodstream: the whole is greater than the sum of its parts.

Unlike most plants and animals, the human body cannot produce this nutrient. The body needs vitamin C daily, either through the ingestion of foods or supplements. The alkaline environment of the intestines may reject vitamin C (water-soluble ascorbic acid) causing tissue inflammation, flatulence, diarrhea, discomfort and, consequently, minimal absorption and rapid elimination of this valuable nutrient. Researchers report that 78–88% of vitamin C intake passes through the body without being absorbed or utilized.

The Superior Vitamin C

IN THE Ester-C® manufacturing process, vitamin C is fully reacted with calcium in a water solution. No organic solvents or precipitation (heat) are used, resulting in a neutral pH, a strong mineral bond and the production of naturally occurring vitamin C metabolites (a property unique to Ester-C®).

Ester-C® is both water and fat soluble. Like water, it is totally non-acidic. Ester-C® is neutralized, making it "stomach friendly." The presence of metabolites makes Ester-C® more bioavailable; it enters the bloodstream and tissues and is used more efficiently at the circulation and tissue levels.

Ester-C® PLUS™ is the ultimate vitamin C. How the Ester-C® tablets are made is what differentiates one tablet manufacturer's product from another. Pure Planet® has taken Ester-C® a step further by fortifying it with nature's richest whole food source: spirulina. The naturally occurring bioflavonoids and wide spectrum of trace minerals in spirulina help the body assimilate and absorb the Ester-C®. Spirulina replaces most of the binders, fillers and tableting aids used in other manufacturers' products and provides a multitude of additional whole food vitamins and nutrients.

Ginseng PLUS™: The King of Herbs Meets the Sacred Power Food of the Aztecs

Ginseng's Roots

GINSENG, meaning the "essence of earth in the form of a man" in Chinese, probably received its name from the shape of its long fleshy root which is the part of the plant containing most of the beneficial properties.

For over five thousand years the Chinese have believed ginseng possesses powerful properties that revitalize and restore balance in the body systems. They included it in their herbal formulas as a cure for cancer, rheumatism, diabetes, sexual debility and aging, and to restore health as well as prolong life. Europeans first heard about the beneficial properties of ginseng in the mid-1600s, from explorers returning from Asia.

Ginseng also grows naturally in North America. Native Americans have long valued the plant's curative properties and its ability to prolong life, and they imbued it with mystical powers. Europeans identified the North American variety in the early 1700s, and when it was recognized to be superior to the Oriental species, Asian demand for American ginseng almost brought about its extinction.

Cultivation of American ginseng began in the late 1800s, and today 95% of the U.S. crop (almost 4 million pounds) is exported to Asia annually.

Reality of the Myth

IN THE PAST, ginseng was regarded as a panacea for many illnesses and a tonic for general health. This so-called myth has withstood the test of time. Ginseng is now regarded as an adaptogen, meaning that it has the ability to help return the body to a normal condition regardless of its state of health or disease. An adaptogen raises the body's tolerance to physical and psychological stress so that the body's systems can maintain balance. Ginseng's ability to regulate stress and improve endurance are examples of its adaptogenic properties.

Ginseng root contains at least 29 active ingredients, or ginsenosides. Of these, the Rb and Rg ginsenosides are perhaps the most significant. Rb_1 has a calming effect on the body (yin qualities), helping it manage stress, while Rg_1 has a stimulating effect (yang qualities), giving the body energy. Not surprisingly, the Chinese recognized these soothing yet revitalizing properties of ginseng, which parallel the balance integral in the Chinese philosophy of yin and yang.

Modern research has identified the following properties in ginseng's ginsenosides:

- Radioprotective
- Antitumor
- Antiviral
- Stabilizes blood sugar levels in hypo-glycemics & diabetics
- Improves athletic performance
- Raises tolerance to physical and psychological stress
- Aphrodisiac
- Antifatigue
- Antistress
- Memory Retention

The Superior Ginseng

ALL TRUE GINSENGS have Panax (the Greek word for panacea or cure-all) as part of their scientific name. *Panax ginseng* from Asia and *Panax quinquefolius* from North America are the two primary forms of true ginseng.

American ginseng root is more potent than the Asian variety because it has a higher concentration of ginsenosides, especially Rb_1 and Rg_1. The ratio of Rb_1 to Rg_1 is 5:1 in American ginseng and only 2:1 in Asian ginseng. Primarily for this reason American ginseng has been found to be more effective than Asian ginseng in stress management, recovery, and controlling high blood pressure. It is more protecting of the adrenal glands and can be taken over a long period of time without causing overuse reactions. Asian ginseng, on the other hand, is more appropriate for short-term stimulation.

For maximum potency, only the root powder from American ginseng (*Panax quinquefolius*) is used in Ginseng PLUS™. Other ginseng products on the market may include the leaf and stem of the plant, which are not as beneficial. Every batch of Ginseng PLUS™ is tested for potency and freshness.

Ginseng PLUS™ is a unique and powerful combination of ginseng, the King of Herbs, in a base of pure spirulina, sacred food of the Aztecs. Ginseng PLUS™ combines the best of the East and the West, a harmonic balance for the body.

Each is a superior product in itself; together they work synergistically to enrich the other's individual qualities and enhance their absorption into the body. The ginsenosides, for example, facilitate the assimilation of spirulina's proteins into the bloodstream. Ginseng PLUS™ provides all the restorative benefits of this ancient panacea... and more.

Amla-C PLUS™— Nature's Most Potent Source of vitamin C

AMLA, INDIA'S GOOSEBERRY, *(Emblica officinalis),* is the best whole food source of vitamin C and naturally occurring bioflavonoids. Research shows that amla is 12 times more assimilable and creates more potent medicinal effects than synthetic vitamin C. For example, one tablet contains 400 mg of amla or 27 mg of natural, bio-available vitamin C which is equivalent to 300 mg of synthetic vitamin C.

Pure Planet® has combined spirulina with amla in a whole food tablet using no tableting aids, binders or fillers. Amla increases protein synthesis, making spirulina, which is 60% protein, a perfect synergistic ingredient. Like amla, spirulina also enhances the immune system. Both are tridosaghna, meaning they are beneficial for all Ayurvedic body types.

Amla contains high levels of the antioxidant Superoxide Dismutase (SOD) and tannins which inhibit the degradation of vitamin C and acts as cellular protective agents against oxidative stress. Many of the great Ayurvedic tonics are based on amla and have been used for centuries as a powerful digestive aid, liver stimulant, antifungal, antibacterial, antihistaminic, antiviral and antacid. It has also been used to increase lean body mass and help with weight management.

The Supernatural Meal™—World's First Complete and Natural Green Meal in a Drink

AFTER MORE than ten years of research, Pure Planet® created this easy-to-use, instant nutritious complete meal. You just add water and shake to create a complete, healthy, delicious meal to enjoy at home or on the go. No juices, fruit or blender needed.

Simple is better. Pure Planet® made it easy for the body to identify, digest and assimilate the meal because, according to nutrition and allergy specialists, the body prefers fewer ingredients in simple formulas consisting of powerful foods.

Spirulina is packed with concentrated nutrients, all working synergistically to provide a boost in energy and vitality while satisfying the appetite. It has more of what matters. The Super-Natural Meal™ delivers ten or more grams of pure spirulina per serving. Most other green formulas contain less than one gram.

Each ingredient has been carefully selected for its synergistic nutritional value as well as superior taste. Our argon gas-flushed SepraPak™ insures absolute freshness by keeping key ingredients separated. This prevents oxidation when sensitive ingredients are mixed or stored in a can or jar.

Organic Instant Rice Milk: Statistics show that most people have at least a slight allergic reaction to cow's milk. In accordance with Pure Planet's desire to support people and the planet in health, no dairy products are used in any of Pure Planet's products. In addition, the rice provides a clean source of nutrition, especially carbohydrates.

Hawaiian Spirulina: Pure Planet's spirulina is grown, harvested and dried with the highest standards of any blue-green algae in the world. It is the best-tasting of all the algae and the ultimate superfood.

Organic Sprouted Barley: Like spirulina, sprouted barley is a live, whole superfood. It is also the best tasting of all the sprouted grains tested at Pure Planet®. It is grown fresh-to-order and air dried at low temperatures, insuring live enzymes and bioavailable nutrients.

Freeze-Dried Raspberry, Strawberry and Blueberry: Berries from whole fruit are nutritionally superior to spray-dried fruit powders. These gourmet, whole dried berries are milled fresh for delicious flavor and are a great source of fiber, vitamins C and A, plus an abundance of minerals.

Organic Flaxseed Meal: Organic flaxseed meal is a prime source of fiber and Omega 3, 6 and 9. It oxidizes rapidly and does not store well unless it is sealed in a gas-flushed envelope. The nutty tasting seeds are ground at low temperatures and packaged with a process which protects the EFA's and other nutrients from damaging light, heat and oxygen exposure.

Amla Berry: The Amla berry has been treasured in India for over 5,000 years for its restorative and balancing influences on the body. In addition to providing numerous antioxidants, bioflavonoids and vitamins, Amla is also the highest natural whole food source of vitamin C.

Organic Maple Granules: Since maple trees grow wild in forests, the organic refers to how maple products are harvested and made. Unlike most maple products, Pure Planet's maple granules are processed without the use of formaldehyde and reducing chemicals.

Lecithin: Soy lecithin is a lipotropic (fat-burning) agent impor tant to many body functions, particularly healthy nerve and cell membranes. It is an excellent source of choline, inositol phosphorus and linoleic acid.

Ester-C®: Ester-C® is another great antioxidant. Ester-C® ascor bate provides a mineral component that is nutritionally essen tial. Ester-C® is gentle to the stomach and non-acidic (neutra pH). It also provides essential calcium.

Green foods are important for vibrant health. Spirulina's green pigment, chlorophyll, has revitalizing and refreshing effects on the body including the ability to detoxify and puri fy the body. Research on phycocyanin, a blue-green pigment documents positive effects on the immune system. Dare to go green!

15
Pure Planet® Spirulina Recipes

CREATING RECIPES with spirulina can be fun, enlivening and tasty. Use spirulina powder in culinary creations, sprinkle it lightly over dinner and salads, and find a new zest and excitement with food. It's easy, nutritious and colorful. In addition to the daily minimum suggested serving of spirulina (ten grams or twenty tablets) and the food plan discussed earlier, consider additional supplementation of vitamin C, folic acid, zinc, calcium, vitamin D (sun), food yeast and the Spirulina Calcium drink:

1 cup soaked, unhulled sesame seeds	6 Tbsp carob
	2 Tbsp honey
1 Tbsp vanilla	1 tsp spirulina
4 cups water	1 banana (optional)

Blend, sieve & enjoy!

Here are a few simple rules to follow:
When first using spirulina powder, use 1 to 2 teaspoonful per recipe to acclimate to the taste. You can always add more later. Add spirulina towards the end of the cooking process, as the most benefit will come the less it is heated. It can be added to any recipe. It is a dry ingredient, so add it to recipes accordingly.

The following recipes are all allergy-free and nutritious. All ingredients are readily available in health food stores and some supermarkets. Enjoy!

Spirulina Potato Chips

6 potatoes	1 tsp cumin powder
3 tsp tamari soy sauce	2 tsp garlic powder
2 tsp paprika	2 tsp spirulina powder

Slice potatoes in long thin strips.
Toss with spices and bake at 375° until browned.

Spirulina Popcorn

Combine with popped popcorn:

2 tsp spirulina powder	3 tsp tamari soy sauce
2 Tbsp brewers yeast	Garlic powder
2 tsp kelp	Olive oil

Mix well. For sweet popcorn, soften 2 tbsp honey and add to other ingredients omitting soy sauce and garlic powder.

Spirulina Dip

1 tbsp ginger	12 soaked almonds (soak overnight, drain & rinse)
2 tsp spirulina powder	
1 cup chopped parsley	1 Tbsp lecithin
6 cloves garlic	1 lemon juiced
3 spring onions, chopped	3 Tbsp tamari soy sauce
enough water to cover	4 Tbsp brewers yeast

Whiz all ingredients in the blender. Chill before serving. Goes well with celery & carrot sticks or healthy chips.

Banana Energy Treats

4 mashed bananas	1 cup coconut
1 cup ground sunflower seeds	2 Tbsp lecithin
½ cup soaked currants	1 tsp vanilla extract
½ cup tahini or almond butter	2 tsp spirulina powder
4 Tbsp soy milk powder	

Combine all ingredients. Make into balls or logs. Roll in coconut and chill.

Garden-Filled Potatoes

4 large baked potatoes	½ tsp chili powder
2 onions diced	2 tsp ginger
1½ cups corn, peas & celery	2 Tbsp chopped fresh basil
2 tsp tamari soy sauce	or 2 tsp dried
2 Tbsp brewers yeast	2 tsp oregano
	1 Tbsp spirulina powder

Cut potatoes in half and scoop out potato from shell.
Sauté remaining ingredients in ½ cup water (except spirulina).
Add the mixture to the potato, then add Spirulina powder.
Put this mixture back in the shell and bake 15 minutes at
400°. Top with Gravy Verde if desired.

Gravy Verde

½ cup rice flour	3 Tbsp brewers yeast
water	4 Tbsp tamari soy sauce
1 tsp cumin powder	5 cloves garlic, pressed
1 Tbsp spirulina powder	

Brown rice flour in pan stirring constantly until slightly
brown. Add water gradually until thick and creamy, stirring
continuously. Add remaining ingredients and simmer for
5–10 minutes. Add more water if necessary. Add spirulina
before serving.

Dilled Beans

½ lb green beans	juice of 1 lemon
1 onion sliced in rounds	12 slivered almonds
¼ cup chopped fresh dill weed	1 tsp spirulina powder

Steam beans & onions for 5 minutes.
Add remaining ingredients and sprinkle spirulina on top.

Avocado Dressing

⅔ cup of water

1 avocado

juice of one lemon

2 Tbsp apple cider vinegar

4 cloves garlic

1 tsp ginger

½ tsp cumin powder

1 Tbsp miso

2 tsp spirulina powder

Whiz together in a blender and serve immediately.
Delicious on a fresh tossed green salad!

Leprechaun Macaroons

Mix in bowl:

4 cups coconut

1 cup sliced almonds

⅔ cup barley flour

½ tsp salt

1 Tbsp spirulina

Add:

1⅓ cups maple syrup

2 tsp almond extract

Form into balls and place on cookie sheet. Bake at 350° for
10 minutes.

Tofu Gravy

1 block tofu

juice of 3 lemons

2 Tbsp paprika

1 Tbsp tamari

3 Tbsp lecithin

⅓ cup brewers yeast

3 Tbsp grated fresh ginger (optional)

1 Tbsp spirulina powder

fresh herbs to taste
i.e. parsley, basil, dill

Blend all ingredients in the blender adding water, if needed,
to acquire a smooth consistency. Heat and serve over
steamed vegetables.

Spirulina Rush ™

8 oz. Chilled, Apple Juice

1 tsp. Spirulina Powder

1 small banana (optional)

Place ingredients in a blender or jar with lid tight and blend or shake until well mixed. Enjoy refreshing, instant energy, and whole food nutrition when taking Pure Planet Spirulina.

Ester-C® PLUS Booster ™

8 oz. Chilled, Fruit Juice of Choice

1/2 tsp. Ester-C ® PLUS Powder

Place ingredients in a blender or jar with lid tight and blend or shake until well mixed. Enjoy refreshing, instant vitamin C energy, and whole food nutrition when taking Pure Planet Ester-C® PLUS™ with Spirulina.

Ginseng PLUS Elixir ™

8 oz. Chilled, Spiced Apple Juice

1 tsp. Ginseng PLUS Powder

Place ingredients in a blender or jar with tight lid and blend or shake until well mixed. Enjoy refreshing, instant energy, and whole food nutrition when taking Pure Planet Ginseng PLUS™ Spirulina.

Power Carob-Mint Shake ™

8 oz. Chilled, Vanilla Rice Milk

1 Tbs. Carob-Mint Powder

Vanilla Ice Cream (optional)

Place ingredients in a blender or jar with lid tight and blend or shake until well mixed. Enjoy refreshing, instant energy, and whole food nutrition when taking Pure Planet Power Carob-Mint Spirulina.

Piné-amla Colada ™

8 oz. Pineapple Coconut Juice

1/2 tsp. Amla Powder

Place ingredients in a blender or jar with lid tight and blend or shake until well mixed. Enjoy refreshing, instant Vitamin C energy, and whole food nutrition when taking Pure Planet Amla-C PLUS™ with Spirulina.

Fruit Medley ™

8 oz. Chilled, Apple or Fruit Juice of Choice

1/2 frozen banana

1/2 tsp. Amla-C PLUS™ Powder

Place ingredients in a blender or jar with lid tight and blend or shake until well mixed. Thirst-quenching, instant vitamin C energy, and whole food nutrition when taking Pure Planet Amla-C PLUS™ with Spirulina.

Tropical C Smoothie ™

8 oz. Chilled, Mango Juice

4 oz. Rice Dream or Vanilla Yogurt

1/2 tsp. Amla-C PLUS™ Powder

Place ingredients in a blender or jar with tight lid and blend or shake until well mixed. Satisfying, instant energy, and whole food nutrition when taking Pure Planet Amla-C PLUS™.

Amla-Banana Shake ™

8 oz. Vanilla Soy or Rice Milk

1 Frozen Banana

1 Scoop of Frozen Vanilla Rice Dream or Frozen Yogurt

1/2 tsp. Amla-C PLUS™ Powder

Place ingredients in a blender with tight lid and blend or shake until well mixed. Delicious, instant energy, and whole food nutrition when taking Pure Planet Amla-C PLUS™.

Bibliography

Carmichael, Wayne W., (1994), *The Toxins of Cyanobacteria*, Scientific American

Challem, Jack J., and Lewin, Renate, *Spirulina: Food of the Future*, Let's Live Magazine

Devi, M. A., et al, *Medical Research with Spirulina*

Henrikson, Robert, (1994), *Earth Food Spirulina, How This Remarkable Blue-Green Algae Can Transform Your Health and Our Planet*

Henson, Ronald, (1995), *Super Foods for Body Defense*

Kallenback, Laurel, (1997), *Health Benefits of Algae*, Delicious!, April

Kay, Robert, Ph.D., RD, *How to Choose the Right Microalgae for You!* Healthy & Natural Journal, vol. 3, no. 3

Kozlenko, Richard, DVM, Ph.D., MPH, and Henson, Ronald H., *The Study of Spirulina, Effects on the AIDS Virus, Cancer and the Immune System* , Healthy & Natural Journal, vol. 3, no. 5

Light, Luise, EdD, Spirulina, *Bread of the Aztecs, Elixir for Today*, Vegetarian Voice

Lloyd, John, *Aqua Farming, The Key to the Purest Blue-Green Algae on the Planet*

Moorhead, Kelly, B*eta Carotene Studies Point to the Importance of Natural Sources*, Cyanotech Corp.

Morgan, Helen C. And Moorhead, Kelly J. (1993), *Spirulina, Nature's Superfood*, 1993, Nutrex, Inc.

Nakaya, N. Et al. (1986), *The Effect of Spirulina on Reduction of Serum Cholesterol*, Tokai University, Japan

O'Connor, Amy, (1996), *Spirulina Spurs Hope*, Vegetarian Times, April 1996

Rector-Page, Linda, ND, Ph.D., *About Green Superfoods*, Healthy Healing, An Alternative Healing Reference, Ninth Edition

Ronore Enterprises, *Comparing the Green Superfoods*

Rosenbaum, Michael E. (Date unknown), V*itamin C New and Improved, The Promise of Ester-C®*, Health World

Rozman, Deborah, (1987), *The Dolphins Discover Spirulina*, The Enlightener, July

Solovitch, Sara, *Spirulina Not Harmful to Small Children*, Kids Health, Mercury News, Oct. 2, 1996

Weiser, Dr. Karl, *Meat. Neat to Eat?*

Wild Oats, Inc. (1996), *Your Guide to Superfoods, Sea Vegetables, Microalgae, Bee Foods & More*, Wild Oats, Inc.

**PURE
PLANET
PRODUCTS**

SPIRULINA —
POWER HEALTH
HANDBOOK

**PURE
PLANET
PRODUCTS**

SPIRULINA —
POWER HEALTH
HANDBOOK

**PURE
PLANET
PRODUCTS**